The Octopus

Alicia C. Alvarez

Copyright © 2019 Expedition Kids, LLC
All rights reserved.

ISBN-10: 1-7335019-0-8
ISBN-13: 978-1-7335019-0-3

Printed in the USA

No part of this publication may be photocopied, reproduced, distributed electronically, or transmitted in any form or by any means (whether electronic or mechanical), without permission in writing from the copyright owner.

ACKNOWLEDGMENTS

Special thanks to my two beautiful blessings and your love for learning; to my husband for his support and reassurance through this new adventure, to my parents for their guidance, and Alyssa for constructive criticism and review. This book would be an idea sitting on a dusty shelf without each of you!

Over 300 kinds of *octopus* live in the sea,
but many more may be found by you and me.

Most do not like water that is very cold,
and many do not live to be very old.

Some live on shallow *reefs* or in deep caves,
while others live life below the warm waves.

Octopuses live mostly alone,
tending to shell gardens of their own.

Octopuses are smart, quick, and flexible,
and are known to be extremely colorful.

They may appear yellow, red, orange, purple, or blue;
some octopuses have neat spot and stripe patterns too.

An octopus can quickly vanish from your sight,
by *contracting* its muscles and reflecting light!

They can fit into almost any sized space,
because octopuses are *invertebrates*!

Octopuses don't have bones or joints;
their arms can bend at several points.

The octopus possesses three working hearts;
some octopus even glow in the dark!

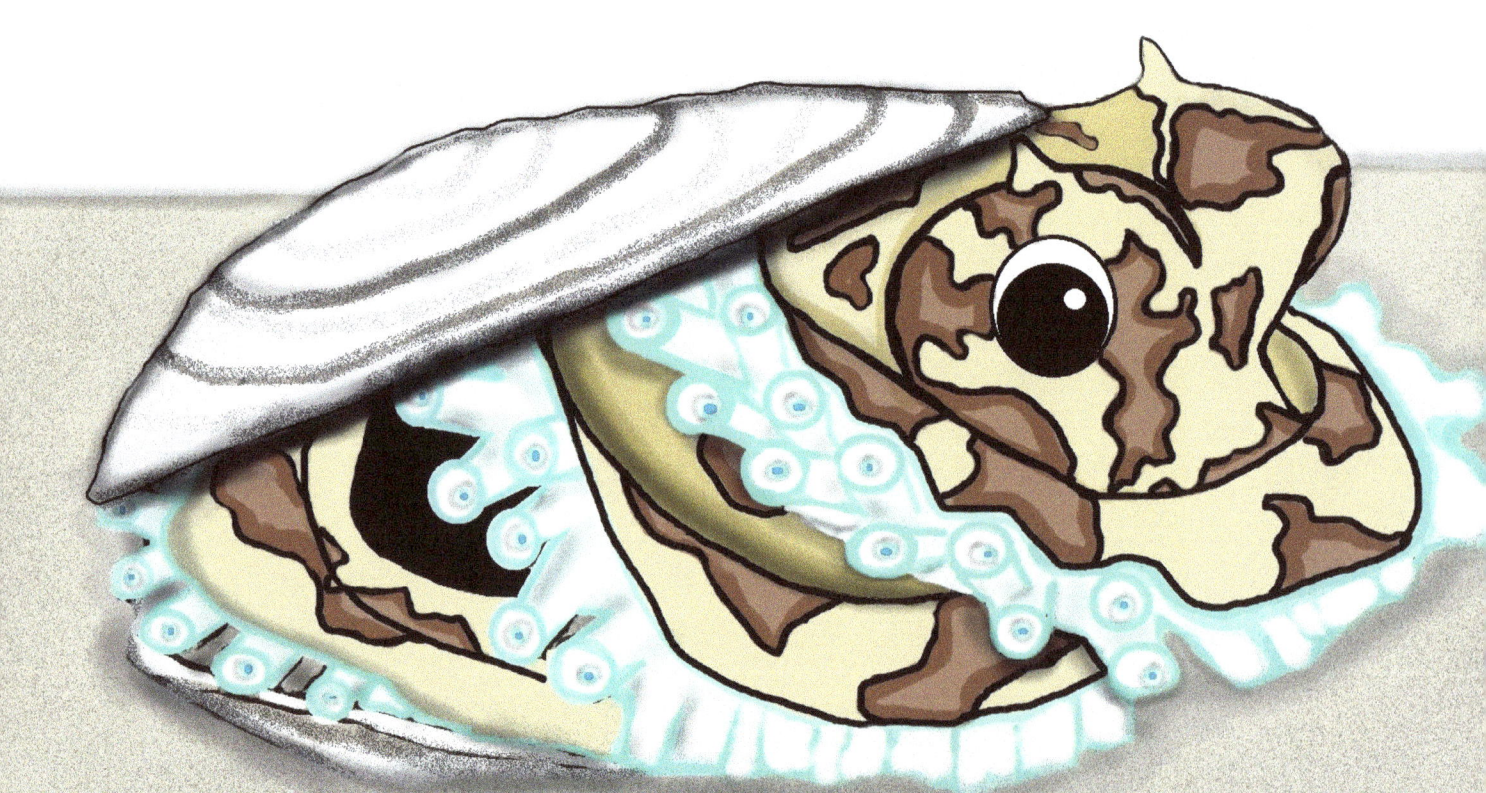

To save energy an octopus rarely swims,
instead, it walks on the bottom using its *limbs*.

When octopuses need to quickly move,
they force water through a specialized tube.

This action quickly propels them back;
it's like having a water jetpack!

Each octopus has a *venomous* bite,
given by a beak it keeps out of sight.

Only one octopus has been found to be deadly,
 and it shows it's yellow skin and blue rings readily.

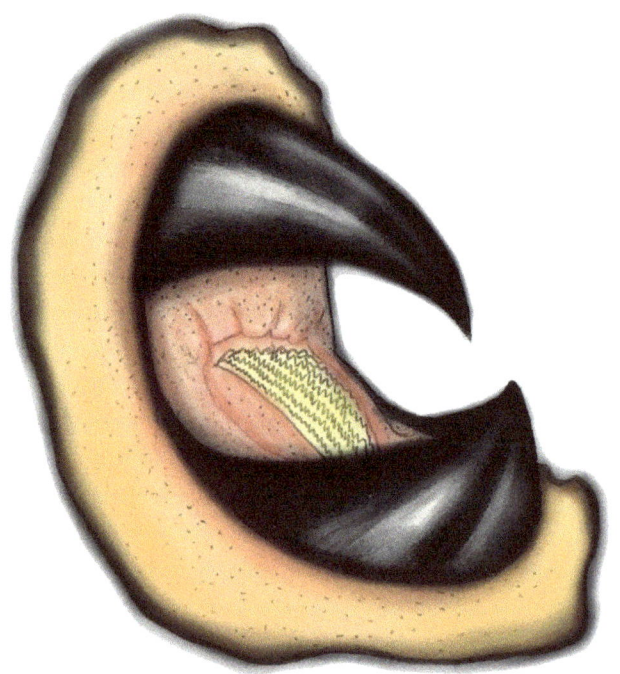

Their many arms can think quickly for themselves,
as they reach for food along the ocean shelves.

Crab, lobster, and shrimp are their favorite things to eat,
it's amazing anything could escape their eight feet!

Hundreds of tiny suction cups allow them to grab and taste,
octopuses basically have tongues all over the place.

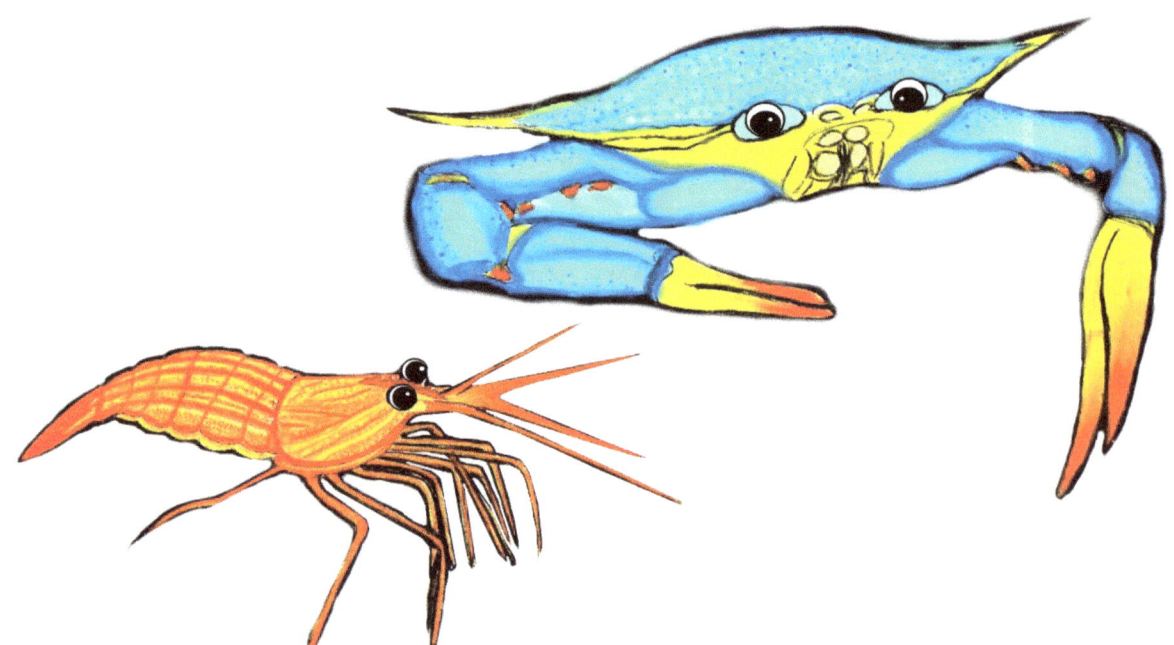

Unfortunately, they can become tasty meals;
they are eaten by humans, whales, birds, fish, and seals.

If it loses an arm from a predatory attack,
the octopus will be okay, and it's arm will grow back!

Octopuses can escape behind a cloud of black, making it difficult for *predators* to attack.

This black ink can dull a predator's sight and sense of smell, allowing octopuses to flee or *camouflage* well.

A mother octopus can lay thousands of eggs in her lair;
she will intensely guard them, clean them, and provide them with air.

Hatching her eggs is an extraordinary feat,
and now a mother octopus' life is complete.

Babies are ready for life on their own,
and float up to the ocean's *plankton zone*.

Later they sink to the ocean floor,
where they will grow and develop more.

Few will grow to have babies of their own,
and now, their cycle of life has been shown.

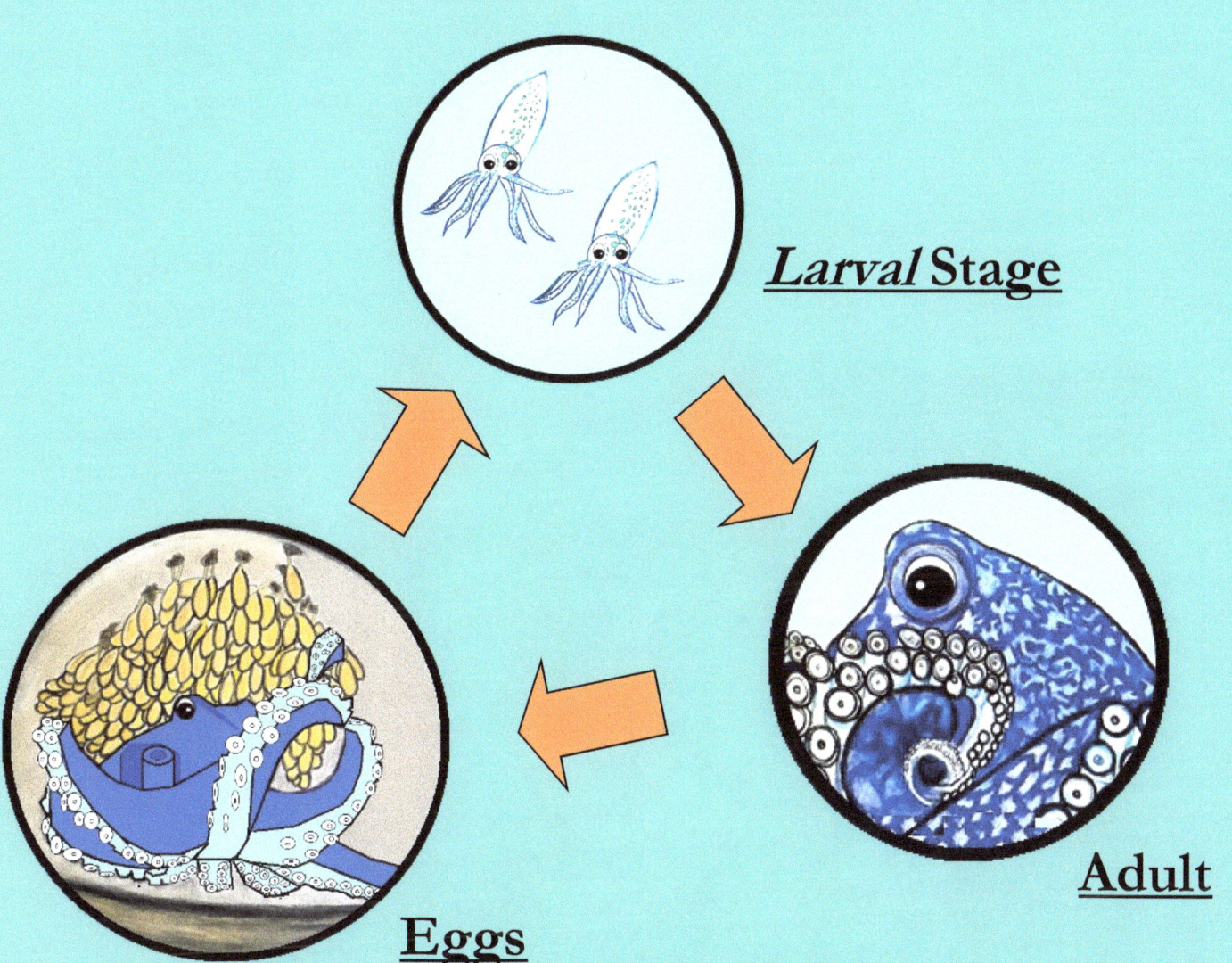

This may be extremely difficult to believe but it's true,
they are related to squid, nautilus, and cuttlefish too!

The current *status* of the octopus is unknown,
but we know that *marine pollution* threatens their home.

Octopuses throughout the world are heavily *pressured*,
let's remind others that they are something to be treasured!

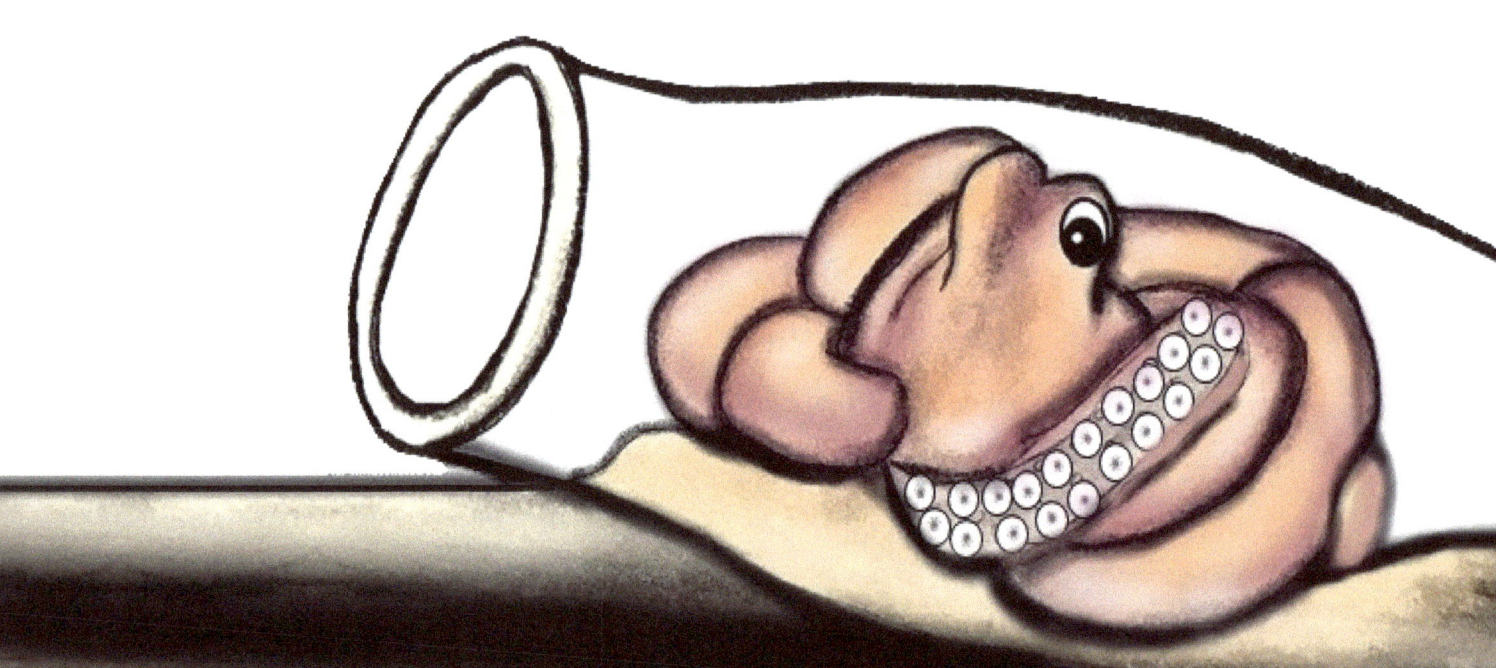

VOCABULARY

Italicized words throughout the book are listed and defined below.

Camouflage: a way an animal is able to hide or blend in with its surroundings. This is most often achieved by using the color or texture of their skin, fur, or scales.

Contract: to make smaller by the act of drawing together, tensing, or tightening.

Invertebrate: an animal that does not have a backbone or spine.

Larval: a name given to a baby or immature animal that hatches from an egg. For example, a caterpillar is considered to be a larval stage for the butterfly.

Limbs: the legs or arms of an animal; an octopus walks along the ocean floor by using its arms.

Marine Pollution: term given to waste or trash that is found in the ocean.

Octopus: a sea animal that is characterized by a soft, oval-shaped body with eight arms that are lined with two rows of suction cups. They do not have any skeleton (or bone) in their bodies, but they have strong beak-like jaws for crushing the shells of their food.

Plankton Zone: the layer of the ocean in which plankton (microscopic organisms), float and drift in the ocean currents.

Predator: an animal that hunts other animals for food.

Pressure: an increase in demand such as harvesting or overfishing, that can result in a smaller population.

Reef: a place where ocean animals live, it can be thought of as an underwater city. These areas are found near or at the surface of the ocean and can be made of rock, coral, sand or other materials (such as a sunken ship).

Status: refers to the health of a population and whether there is great potential for the population to go extinct (die off), or for the population to stay healthy and live on.

Venomous: an animal that can make venom (a harmful toxin or poison). Venom is often used as a form of protection when an animal bites or stings something that it is afraid of. However, some animals use their venom as a way to catch their food.

VISIT OUR WEBSITE

Please visit our website www.ExpeditionKids.org. It is our goal to provide additional materials and fun activities that promote interactive learning. Each book will be accompanied by free printable workbooks that include fun facts, vocabulary words, maps, diagrams, creative projects, puzzles, and more.

Lightning Source UK Ltd.
Milton Keynes UK
UKHW020912101220
374878UK00002B/75